ROME'S
Female SAINTS

A Poetic Pilgrimage to the Eternal City

Nicol Nixon Augusté, PhD

D1328440

WESTBOW
PRESS®
A DIVISION OF THOMAS NELSON
& ZONDERVAN

The Catholic Study Bible. Second Ed. NAB. Oxford UP, 2011.

WestBow Press books may be ordered through booksellers or by contacting:

WestBow Press
A Division of Thomas Nelson & Zondervan
1663 Liberty Drive
Bloomington, IN 47403
www.westbowpress.com
1 (866) 928-1240

ISBN: 978-1-5127-8177-9 (sc)
ISBN: 978-1-5127-8178-6 (e)

Library of Congress Control Number: 2017906929

Print information available on the last page.

WestBow Press rev. date: 03/14/2018

For André

Saints were remarkable because no one saw them coming.

~ Rev. Jerome Santamaria, Rome, 2016[1]

There is no hidden poet in me, just a little piece of God that might grow into poetry.

~ Etty Hillesum, *An Interrupted Life*

Nihil Obstat   *Father Pablo M. Migone*

Chancellor & Vocation Director

Diocese of Savannah

Imprimatur   *Most Reverend Gregory J. Hartmayer, OFM Conv.*

Bishop of Savannah

Contents

The backstory of this project originally involved researching the narratives of first-century women who worshipped and sacrificed their lives for the Jewish-Christian God. However, the more time I spent studying in Rome, Italy, the more I began to truly engage with—and fall in love with—The Eternal City. This project organically evolved into a multidisciplinary work that celebrates female saints associated with Rome. My research took me to impressive libraries, including the Arthur & Janet C. Ross Library and the Vatican Library. I visited Rome's numerous spectacular churches, sites of martyrdom, archeological areas, and captivating catacombs. Also, I was afforded the opportunity to study her stunning sculptures and remarkable reliquaries.

This book includes an entry for each female saint; each entry offers the reader several gems: a brief biographical snapshot of the woman of God, the research site in Rome or Vatican City associated with the saint, and original poetry that celebrates the saint. Also, you will find the Word(s) God gave me while in prayer at the particular research site; this Word from the Lord can be found in the poem dedicated to the saint.

For a more interactive experience, see photo albums for each saint at https://www.facebook.com/romesfemalesaints.

It was not until almost the mid-thirteenth century when the Catholic Church created a formal canonization process for sainthood candidacy. During the early centuries of Christian history, "believers instinctively honored the martyrs in an extraordinary way. And veneration was an almost exclusive privilege of the martyrs. We know of very few *non*-martyr saints from the first three centuries."[2] Normally, when a martyr or another deservedly holy person died, the day of death became that person's day to be claimed and named a saint (now celebrated as feast days).[3] The process gradually changed with time, but became more solidified when in 1234 Pope Gregory IX "established procedures to investigate the life of a candidate saint and any attributed miracles."[4]

From that point, the process evolved into what it is today. The current canonization method involves varied investigations of extraordinary characteristics: miracles associated with the candidate, a lack of heresy or "purity in doctrine," the cause of martyrdom (if applicable), or other motivation for Church and God. Achieving the title of Blessed means the candidate has been validated as a martyr or the candidate has been "credited with a [verified] miracle"; to achieve the title of Sainthood, the Blessed needs one more authenticated miracle.[5] In other words, while non-martyr candidates need two miracles to achieve sainthood, martyrs need only one.

The types of saints explored in this book include Red Crown Martyrs, Doctors of the Church, Forerunners, and Foundresses. Red Crown martyrs are those women whose blood was shed because of their Christian beliefs. Some examples include

Agatha, Cecilia, and Prisca. Doctors of the Church are women such as Catherine of Siena whose work represents remarkable theological wisdom and insight. Forerunners embody women who helped to usher in Jesus Christ and His ministry, including Mary Mother and Mary Magdalene. Foundresses represent those women who founded religious orders, giving their lives to evangelize Christ. Women in this category include women such as Frances and Teresa of Calcutta.

ON THE WORD MARTYR

The word martyr actually means "witness" in the Greek language. While the word's history was primarily used in the legal field, it did not see its current usage until the second century of the Christian or Common Era: before "[second century] Christian literature...[the word martyr] had never designated dying for a cause. When it finally assumed that sense, its meaning of 'witness' began to slip away, so that the word 'martyr' in Greek and the same word borrowed in Latin came more and more to mean what it means today."[6] Here, the act of dying can express different meanings, leading to titles such as red crown martyrs and white crown martyrs, titles that still apply today. Red crown martyrs die through the shedding of blood at the hands of another person because of a belief in Christ. White crown martyrs die to the world's whims and fleshly desires; these white crowns "willingly [give] up worldly concerns and [make] his or her life a perpetual pilgrimage. A white [crown] martyr lives a life of heroic devotion for Him alone, eagerly uniting that devotion with Christ's sufferings."[7] The majority of the women in this book represent red crown saints, but there are others included that could be considered white crown saints.

While other early cultures teemed with male heroes, "Christians actually made women themselves their epic heroes…the hero was not a man who flashed his sword in battle, but a woman who just stood there and accepted death for the sake of Christ."[8] Women endured especially cruel treatment. Whether single or married, these women chose a life of Christian holiness. Although this choice to follow Christ came with gendered benefits, it also potentially came with the cost of martyrdom: "the choice of Christian virginity gave a woman a power nothing else in the ancient world gave her. It gave her the right to be defined as a *person*, not as a man's possession. She belonged to Christ alone, and in Christ there is neither male or female (1 Cor. 3:23)…[Even] for a noble-woman from a rich family, it might be the only way to be *herself*—to make a choice about what was really important in her life."[9] Knowing that many Christian women lived lives of purity, some accounts suggest torturers used a variety of methods to publically mock these women of faith: iron branding, burning, continuous rape until death, and/or hours of public nudity (via hanging by one foot, the hair, or other means) in order to send a message of scorn to Christ followers.[10]

ON RELICS

Relics have fascinated people for centuries. A relic can be categorized into three classes: first-class relics are parts of a saint's body. Second-class relics represent a saint's clothing or an item the person used. Third-class relics represent objects that have touched a first class relic.[11] While several religions use relics, the Catholic tradition has been honoring these items since the early martyr era. By honoring, I do not mean worshipping. Just as all Christians worship the Creator (and not the creation), those who revere relics worship the Creator the relic points to (not the actual object). The relic is honored as a remembrance of a person's witness/martyrdom/devotion to Christ. The relic itself contains no power; its presence ultimately signifies God's power. Therefore, when miracles involving relics occur, it is God performing the miracle, not the relic.

Historically, early Christians would keep relics such as the remains (or ashes of those people burned alive), clothing, or other items to bury or keep in order to venerate that person's commitment to Christ. Early Christians gathered together at burial sites like catacombs and other places to commemorate a saint's Call from God to holiness and sacrifice. Followers of Christ would have known these sties well, and some would have even requested to be buried near a saint. The legalization of Christianity in 313 CE due to Roman emperor Constantine's *Edict of Milan* would bring with it the building of public spaces such as churches and basilicas as well as the transference of saint's bodies and/or associated relics to those sites. It was "vital that the Christian community keep those remains in control…By keeping all the bodily remains of a saint under the control of the whole Christian community of a town or city, as represented by its bishop, and by making them available to all through the building of a public basilica, episcopal and ecclesiastical authority was strengthened and the private appropriation of relics avoided."[12] This practice helped to stave off fraud and theft, but was not always successful.

Today, these relics remain a large part of the Catholic culture, especially in Rome. Inquiries involving the relics' authenticity still remain today; however, this is a topic for another work entirely. Christians are not forced to honor a relic, so if that relic is "spurious, no dishonor is done to God by the continuance of an error which has been handed down in perfect good faith for many centuries. On the other hand the practical difficulty of pronouncing a final verdict upon the authenticity...must be patent to all."[13]

Acknowledgements

Thank you for your engagement with and excitement for this project:

André Augusté, my husband and artistic collaborator; the people who lovingly supported this endeavor at home and abroad; the Savannah College of Art and Design; the American Academy in Rome; the Bishop's Office for U.S. Visitors to the Vatican; The Lay Centre at Foyer Unitas; and, the kind people of Rome.

I

RED CROWN MARTYRS

The blood of the martyrs is the seed of the church.

~ Tertullian

A gatha

Feast Day, February 5

Patron saint of breast cancer patients and sexual assault victims, Agatha (d. 251CE) was born of noble lineage, and was known for her Sicilian beauty and holy purity. She repeatedly refused marriage offers from Quintianus, a local government official and non-Christian. At her continued rejection, he became enraged. He publicly accused her of refusing to worship the local gods, a crime all Christians shared. Guilty, Agatha faced a variety of tortures many other early martyrs also encountered: attempted rape (continuous rape was a common death sentence for Christian virgins), the rack, scourging with hooks, public nudity, and baths comprised of live coals and pottery shards.[14]

Agatha is best known for her miraculous prison healing from a forced double mastectomy. Saint Peter is said to have healed her body completely.[15]

† "Justice" was inspired while praying at Sant'Agatha dei Goti (Saint Agatha of the Goths). The Holy Spirit gifted me with the words deflower, victory, and amazon. This poem is dedicated

to Natalia, a very kind woman who works at the Basilica di Santo Stefano al Monte Celio (Basilica of Saint Stephen in the Round), for the time she spent teaching me about Rome's women of God and for her appreciation of Agatha.

Justice

for Natalia

an original amazon
I am sleek, Sicilian, secreting
blood from my breasts
rather than milk,

deflowered not.

seductive virtue creates
diligence even Saint Peter
can't ignore

my dank prison

clothes me with virtuous victory
against enraged, stank face
judge who would eat my noble fare
like a Great White devours a seal

denied, again.

he draws me a steaming bath
of hot coals and sharp shards,
delighting in my death roll, only to
see me rise, a firewalker!

 A gnes

Feast Day, January 21

Patron saint of virgins and rape victims, Agnes (d. 304CE) is probably the most renowned virgin martyr in the martyrology. At age 12 or 13, Agnes consecrated her virginity to Christ rather than marry. One rejected suitor—a prefect's son who refused to control his emotions—decided to freely reveal her identity as a Christ follower. Convicted, she (like many other virgins) faced sexual assault. But Agnes was saved! The ill-intentioned offender was stricken blind! But rather than seeing his punishment as fit for his intent Agnes prayed for the man, and his sight was immediately restored.

Jacobus de Voragine's *The Golden Legend* tells a very sensational tale that names the prefect's son as that malevolent man; in that account, he was struck dead before being brought back to life via Agnes's prayers. Agnes faced a public burning; however, the flames did not engulf her, parting at her feet. She gained martyrdom by means of beheading, a quick death afforded only to Roman citizens.

On a related note, the blessing of the pallia occurs on her feast day. Pallia are y-shaped wool vestments signifying the clerical commitment unto death, reflecting Christ's (The Good Shepherd) sacrifice to lay down His life for His sheep. The making of the pallia commences with a special ceremony where "red and white crowns are placed on the heads of the lambs as they are prepared to be blessed and sheared."[16]

† "Betrothed" was inspired while praying at Chiesa di Sanctae Agnetis in Agone (Church of Saint Agnes at the Circus Agonalis), where I saw Agnes's very tiny skull. The Holy Spirit gifted me with the word chaos.

Betrothed

purity of a tween, power of a torrent
my virginity parts Vesta's
fire, blinds her rapist's
desire, inspires history's

writers: I am
Ambrose's soulful song
Augustine's constant query
Aurelius's mystical muse

an oracular agent for my future Jewish
sister Frank, firmly we
stand in thick, lovely
divine chaos, chatting
somewhere in

veritas,

verifying miracles, vivifying
matrimony, viewing
martyrdom,
happily inciting love.

nastasia of Rome and Basilissa of Rome

Feast Day, April 15

Persecuted and martyred under Emperor Nero around 68CE, both Saint Anastasia and Saint Basilissa of Rome were of noble Roman lineage. These brave women were known throughout the Christian community for helping to bury the bodies of the martyrs, including their beloved mentors, Apostles Peter and Paul. Once Nero heard the news they had buried the bodies of these leaders of the Way (Christianity), he commanded their deaths by order of scourging with straps, scourging with hooks, burning, and beheading.[17]

† "Burial Practices" was inspired while at the Basilica Papale di San Pietro in Vaticano (Basilica of Saint Peter in the Vatican), Vatican City, while looking up at the Egyptian obelisk, a structure standing approximately 135 feet high that was originally transported from Egypt to Rome by Emperor Caligula (37-41CE). These grounds, later known as Nero's Circus (after Emperor Nero, 54-68CE), served as an initial site where early Christ followers suffered torture, beheadings, and crucifixion; these grounds also saw Christians used as human torches to light Nero's evening events. It was here where the Holy Spirit gifted me with the word hot.

Burial Practices

no time to cry

seeing each other's dusty dry ducts
under clear moonlight kissing
the tip of the 12-story obelisk,

they look down at Peter, or,
what used to be Peter.

nails won't budge from the wood,
blood marries sweat,
forming double helix rivers running
down their soiled, hot arms

"They're coming! We'll have to leave
his feet!"
one whisper-screams to the other

we can't, can we?

a low voice behind them
breaks the darkness, as
a moonlit blade
gleams, striking
like lighting
powerfully parting the

two women
jump back,
gasp
as their sister
forcefully swipes,
then,

just
silence

"He's free," the third Person softly speaks.

six arms hold their beloved,
carrying him to his grave
like a newborn to his crib

Grace thanks them,
perfuming his decaying body

Anastasia of Sirmium

Feast Day, December 25

Patron saint of martyrs, those afflicted with poison, and weavers, Anastasia of Sirmium (d. 304CE) is one of the seven female saints listed and read in the Roman cannon of the Mass recited on Christmas Day; the other six female saints include Agatha, Agnes, Cecilia, Lucy, Felicity and Perpetua. Anastasia was forced to marry a non-Christian, Publius, and refused to consummate their marriage; instead, she focused her attention on imprisoned Christians, a group that would later include her mentor, Saint Chrysogonus. Enraged at her "extra-marital" activity Publius ordered her death, but died before he could carry out his plan.

Later, when found guilty (again) of practicing Christianity, she was sent to capital pontiff Upian, who attempted to sexually assault her. Not only did his attempt fail, but it also left him blind and physically convulsive, prompting him to take his own life. Some legends suggest she was martyred by fire in Sirmium. Others claim she was sent adrift with 200 other virgins for the island of Palmaria, where she would receive her red crown of martyrdom. Her remains were buried in Saint Apollonia's home, a location that would later become a basilica.

† "Adoration Chapel" was inspired while praying at the Basilica of Santa Anastasia Al Palatino (Basilica of Saint Anastasia on Palatine Hill). The Holy Spirit gifted me with the word family.

Adoration Chapel

my silent predawn walk to the prison
is my favorite time of day. Cool
mist kisses my forehead, a sweet
moment that reminds me of my childhood,

that is,

before the rising eastern sun
creates comingling droplets of
purity mixing with maturity,
sweet with sweat.

left to my thoughts,
the joys of a juvenile girl
now rest in the past,
the stony dirt road mourns
under my feet,
my family awaits
my arrival. I am
mother,
sister,
daughter,
father,
brother,
son

in their chapel
they sing until
guards grumble,

apes cage
them until their
fates knock: I watch
roasting
boiling
scourging
severing

for now I pause with them,

rejoicing
in the Risen One,

tendering them my goodbye
until tomorrow's adoration

A ntonina of Nicaea

Feast Day, March 1 (Orthodox)

A virgin living in Bithynia (Turkey), Antonina of Nicaea suffered greatly under Emperor Diocletian (ca. 303-311CE) for her Christian faith. Sources disagree on the classification of her death: one cites beating and burning;[18] another claims beheading;[19] yet another declares death by drowning.[20] What is for certain is that this young woman served as a model of martyrdom—whether she endured the rack for three days or remained imprisoned for two years, her life ended in tremendous suffering, yet in splendid victory.

† "Three Days" was inspired while praying at Chiesa di San Biagio degli Armeni/San Biaglio della Pagnotta (Church of Saint Blaise of the Armenians), where I saw Saint Antonina's relics. The Holy Spirit gifted me with the word wisdom. This poem is dedicated to Sister Bibianna and Sister Rocio, two very joyful, gracious nuns serving at the church.

Three Days

for Sr. Bibianna and Sr. Rocio

from my platform
of martyrdom, I make
eye contact with a
a woman quietly
weeping
from the crowd's
center.
She looks unfamiliar.

for three days, the woman
has stayed with me,
starved
with me,
ached
with me,
choked
with me

on hate and hard
bits of
dirt

lodged
in between

my teeth imprint my sore,
parched inner cheeks

I slump, my knees collapse
her dark, swollen eyes don't avert;
they comfort my discomforting
situation that can only end
in one way,

our hearts fettered,
tethered victory, a
gendered crown
we share

B arbara

Feast Day, December 4

Patron saint of military buildings, firefighters, and all things military and artillery, this third-century virgin saint could be seen as a proto-Rapunzel. Because of her beauty, Barbara's father Dioscorus kept her in a high tower. Not completely alone, orators, philosophers, and poets taught her; through these teachings she decided to convert from polytheism to the monotheistic faith called Christianity.

While Barbara's father was away on a trip, she instructed the builders working on her bath house to construct three windows rather than two, signifying the Triune God. When her father returned, he learned of her conversion and denounced her. Saved from his first homicidal attempt, Barbara was miraculously relocated to a mountain. Her safety would not last, as her father would retrieve her. Her red crown would be achieved via beheading. Shortly after, Barbara's father was struck by lightning, instantly incinerated.

† "A Daughter's Love" was inspired while praying at Santa Barbara dei Librari (Saint Barbara in the Library). This church makes up for its small size with its great beauty. When the light

shines through the window above the Chapel of The Crucifix, located to the right of the main altar, the sight is quite awe inspiring. Just like the windows in Barbara's narrative, this church allows the light to shine through: the light of beauty, the light of love, the light of the Trinity. The Holy Spirit gifted me with the word providential.

A Daughter's Love

Christ's Rapunzel
enclosed in her rock,
in the economy of God
in the arms of philosophy, of poetry,
she rests, thanks be to God!

she has no shelter from the storm
of her punishing father,
her paternal executioner,

save His caressing palm
leaf musing in her hand

patient, she awaits her king's arrival,
slowly, gracefully letting down her
bloody hair and bruised neck,
accepting her providential
crown, her scripted invitation
into eternity

Cecilia

Feast Day, November 22

Patron saint of music, Cecilia (d. 230CE) is known for singing to Christ in her heart and, in response, hearing a heavenly song on the day of her forced wedding to Valerian, a non-Christian. Not only would she retain her virgin status (her holy commitment to Christ), but she also would aid in the conversion of both her husband (who was privileged to see her guardian angel!) and his brother Tiburtius.

The three worked tirelessly for Christ: the brothers buried martyrs' bodies; Cecilia evangelized. Once discovered, all three endured martyrdom. Cecilia survived a series of martyrdom attempts: suffocation in the baths (like a sauna times seven), drowning, and a beheading. During her last three days of life (after an unsuccessful beheading), she continued praying for and preaching to others, and pledging all her earthly effects to the poor.

Notable is the fact that Cecilia's body was found incorrupt during a 1599 excavation. She is the Catholic Church's first incorruptible saint.

† "Love Song" was inspired while praying at Santa Cecilia in Trastevere (Saint Cecilia in Trastevere). The Holy Spirit gifted me with the words especially and loved. "Love Song" is dedicated to Avery Daniel, a very erudite, spirited seminarian studying at the Pontifical North American College (PNAC) in Rome, Italy. He explained the historical significance of as well served as a guide to Cecilia's original burial crypt inside the Catacombs of St. Callixtus.

Love Song

for Avery

my flesh destroyed
my heart warms for you, Lord
you are my triumph,
you are my song

especially loved,
especially bound

I look at you,
smile at your emissary
protecting me
as I rise
up

especially loved,
especially bound

from the fire, the water, the metal
kissing the elements in coolness with wet
lips,
assurance of heaven

freedom! oh God, freedom!
especially loved,
especially bound

the trinity of cuts in my neck
never scar

especially loved,
especially bound

Cecilia's Haiku

Holy Spirit scent
new Eve sings, un-oxidized
in Trastevere

C irilla/Cyrilla

Feast Day, October 28

Martyred during the persecutions of Claudius II (268-270CE), Saint Cirilla (Cyrilla) is known, in part, because of her mother's conversion to Christianity. Tryphonia (her mother) converted after seeing her husband—Cirilla's father and Caesar Decius—die of demonic possession. The next day, her mother would follow her father in death. Known for her charitable heart and for working with the poor, Cirilla refused to marry, telling her suitors that her husband was Jesus, the King of Kings. For this answer, she, like many Christian virgins, would receive her red crown of martyrdom.

† "Roman Holiday" was inspired while praying at the Basilica di Santa Maria in Cosmedin (Basilica of Saint Mary in Cosmedin), also known for the popular "Mouth of Truth" statue, where tourists test their honesty by sticking a hand into the mouth of the Roman river god; if the person proves to be dishonest, the god bites off the person's hand! The crypt under the altar, rediscovered in 1717, boasts ancient marble pillars leading to a small sacrificial alter. Saint Cirilla's relics rest underneath this alter.[21] The Holy Spirit gifted me with the word truth.

Roman Holiday

to know my name is to
bleed parchment and place remnants
of bones in the hole of
Hercules.
We remain here
in memoriam, my
name
representing the poor
of identity
so they can be
remembered by tourists
sticking their hands
in the mouth of
truth only
to be
gnawed with jaws of
deception

F elicity

Patron saint of martyrs, widows, and parents who have lost children to death, Felicity (ca.101-165CE) is famous for her dedication to Christ and martyrdom. Widowed and wealthy, Felicity was considered a real catch during her time. Though, rather than remarry—and gain a father for her seven children— she and her sons continued living lives for Christ; their example helped to convert many people to the faith.

Once the news of their worship and holy example traveled to the second-century emperor, Antonius Pius, they were accused and convicted. Her son's executions—Januarius's whipping, Felix and Philip's beatings, Silvanus's drowning, and Alexandar, Vitalis, and Martial's beheadings—are well known to history. Felicity would drink her own cup of martyrdom via beheading.

† "A Seed of Her Church" was inspired while praying at the Flavian Amphitheatre (otherwise known as the Colosseum/ Coliseum) in Rome. The Holy Spirit gifted me with the word resilient.

A Seed of Her Church

relentless, resilient
against reckless
accusers,
bears
with
blades
stand on hind legs
without insight,
without compassion

fear and peace cannot
lie
together
in a c r y p t

her heart rejoices in her
young son resting
next to
her
arms
eternally
bound round his,
their crowns entwined
with living blood

Julitta

Feast Day, June 16

A mother who fled the Maximian persecution in Lycaonia with her three-year-old (some sources claim three-month-old) son Quiricus, Julitta (d. 304CE) would run not into the arms of tolerance and peace, but into the clutches of cruelty and martyrdom. Both mother and son were arrested and tortured in front of Alexander, the local prefect. Julitta faced flogging; her son, blunt force trauma to the head.

Another source cites that the boy was martyred by flogging, tongue extraction, pan burning (imagine a human-sized frying pan), and blunt force trauma. Julitta would perish from scourging with hooks, hot tar immersion, and beheading.

† "Life's Little Gifts" was inspired while praying at Chiesa di Santa Maria Antiqua al Foro Romano (Ancient Church of Saint Mary in the Roman Forum). Within the walls of the Roman Forum, this sixth-century restored church was recently reopened to the public in 2016, after a 30 year closure. This site serves as one of the earliest Christian monuments inside the Forum; it was resurrected in 1900, after being buried due to an earthquake in 847. The interior of the church boasts a myriad of

frescoes depicting early Christian life, saints, popes, as well as one of the earliest icons of Virgin and Child in Christendom.[22] The preservation effort offers an outstanding interactive presentation allowing viewers to see a full-fresco recreation telling the story of this church as well as those depicted in the frescoes, including the martyrdoms of Julitta and Quiricus. The Holy Spirit gifted me with the word revealed.

Life's Little Gifts

my arms trembled the first time
I held you, covered in blood,
fluid, and love.
Soon my son,
your crown will come

my eyes welled up
watching you sleep, your tiny,
sweet face smiling, cooing
on my breast, talking
with angels and Jesus, I could
almost understand your language.
Soon my son,
your crown will come

your smell made me
love you more,
breathing
in
your
infant
scent,
fresh
to the world from
heavenly places where jasmine
wafts and whispers reveal truths.

Soon my son,
your crown will come

I will not look away from your
crying eyes, filled with terror
and anguish,
your burned arms
reach, and scream for
me, before they fall
limp

my open mouth makes
no sound, I pray
for your
executioner.
Now my son,
your crown has come

Prisca

Feast Day, January 18

Given the ultimatum to either worship the sun deity Apollo or face death, Prisca happily chose death. This virgin martyr served as a spectacle of miraculous martyrdom. During her spoken refusal to worship Apollo, she began to radiate a bright light. Then, a hungry, ferocious lion meant to devour her instead lay at her feet! Prisca's martyrdom would occur via scourging with hooks, burning, and a beheading outside the city walls.

† "Other" was inspired while praying at Santa Prisca (Saint Prisca). Many scholars believe the church is named not for the virgin martyr, but for Priscilla, Paul's friend. This church is a titular church, meaning the church was named after the person who owned the property of the home church (in this case, Foundress Prisca). Sources suggest that Peter stayed here for a while. Excavations have discovered the church was built over a fourth- or fifth-century Mithraeum or temple used to worship the deity Mithras, god of an early mystery cult. Saint Prisca's (Priscilla's) relics are located in the crypt alter. The Holy Spirit gifted me with the phrase, ethos of light.

Other

I committed the crime called atheism
against their sun,

my tallow-scorched flesh torn
from my sides like barbeque
from the bone
licked by my executioner's chops

starving is the easy part

sustaining my lord, the Son:
my aloe, my balm
cries with me,

he whispers in his ethos of light:
my woman, my heart, my Other, my Other
receive my crown, my love, my Other

Seraphia and Sabina

Feast Days: Seraphia, September 3; Sabina, August 29

Although Sabina is the noble woman of this second-century narrative (and has a basilica on Aventine Hill named for her), it is Seraphia, her Syrian slave, who serves as the shining heroine of the story. Seraphia fled to Italy during the Christian persecution. She gave away all she had to the poor, and sold herself into servitude, to the noble woman Sabina. Seraphia would convert her mistress in private, but endured public humiliation and beheading for her faith in Christ. Sabina buried Seraphia in the noble family tomb; this act exposed her own faith as a Christian. Sabina, too, would suffer beheading, following her servant into the Gates of Heaven.

† "On Aventine Hill" was inspired while praying at Basilica di Santa Sabina (Basilica of Saint Sabina). This fifth-century basilica was built on grounds that included Saint Sabina's home site, and boasts a stunning view of Rome. Part of the church was built over a temple dedicated to Juno, as evidenced by the Roman column in the fenced-off deep opening in the floor of the church. The real highlight of this church is a small carving

on the outside wooden door depicting one of the earliest representations of the crucified Jesus; before this portrayal, Jesus was represented as the Good Shepherd. The Holy Spirit gifted me with the word confession.

On Aventine Hill

stepping away from the temple,
I turn from my beloved
Juno:
queen of the gods,
queen of Rome,
queen of me,

into your arms I run, my slave,
an Antiochian refugee
penniless, persistent
passionate,
protective
of me

I quietly repeat your
confession, my sinner's prayer,
your lips tremble, my voice cracks

at the crossroads, the sound
of That name, His name
releases us,

leaving one woman for
another, you are
the Other
of me

S usanna

Feast Day, August 11

Niece of Pope Caius and cousin to Emperor Diocletian, Susanna (d. ca. 290/295CE) came from a house truly divided. When she refused to marry her cousin's adopted, non-Christian son Maxentius Galerius, her suitor tried forcing her to sacrifice to Jupiter at the Roman forum. She refused. Her cousin Diocletian found out, and ordered her death as well as the deaths of all other Christ followers in the family.

All perished, save the Pope (he hid out in the catacombs). Susanna was beheaded in her home. If Maxentius Galerius's name sounds familiar it is because he did end up succeeding Diocletian, but would fall (literally, mortally from the Milvian Bridge into the Tiber River!) to Constantine who would become emperor, legalizing Christianity in 313 CE and making the faith the state religion.

† "A Family Affair" was inspired while standing outside Chiesa di Santa Susanna (Church of Saint Susanna). The Holy Spirit gifted me with the word closed.

A Family Affair

heavy black clouds collect over her
stone house.

Storm's coming.

across the cityscape

a change in the air,
a stench of twelve-day-old refuse:
body parts, entrails, and evil
rise from future ruins
where Jupiter eternally
rests, a lonely old man.

Looking upon
the pediment of the great temple
no regrets of old gods, their decaying
voices disappear
in the wind

she was never one to listen anyway

foreboding, fanatical family
event, closed to the public
today.

This
beheading
isn't meant to
entertain the collective
Roman psyche
or make an example of her
kind,

no matter,
she claims
the lineage, victorious

Vittoria

Feast Day, December 23

Vittoria/Victoria's (d. 304CE) is a story of two sisters. She and her sister Anatolia (also a red-crown saint) were espoused to marry two non-Christian men, Eugenius and Aurelius, respectively. The sisters refused, and were immediately placed on permanent house arrest. Rather than rotting in their captors' prisons, they flourished: they evangelized Jesus Christ and converted the servants and guards! Their betrothed men eventually gave up hope, but never gave up their anger, as both sisters were martyred. Victoria's martyrdom occurred by means of stabbing; Liliarcus, Victoria's state-appointed executioner, contracted leprosy and perished within six days after Victoria's death.

† "Morning in Prison" was inspired while praying at Chiesa di Santa Maria della Vittoria (Church of Our Lady of Victory), where I saw Vittoria encased in clear glass, showing the cuts to her throat and a stab mark to her heart. The Holy Spirit gifted me with the word stunning.

Morning in Prison

early dawn sun
speaks forth her stunning
rays into the prison
where I
spread His light

silent, cold concrete
yet to be warmed
captures my theoretical thoughts,
arrests my mystical memories,
remembers my honeyed heart

How will it be today, Lord?

sitting at his feet,
I am a Mary,

reaching for his hand
breathing in his words
waiting on the guard
who deeply admires
his bird
doing time
in my sacred cage

II

DOCTORS OF
THE CHURCH

Mystical experiences are not intended to replace sound theology. Rather they are the experiential outgrowth of sound theology, infusing it with life and connecting to the very core of our being.

~ John Michael Talbot, *The Way of the Mystics*

C atherine of Siena

Feast Day, April 29

Born on the Feast of the Annunciation, Catherine (1347-1380), grew into one of the most beloved mystics and Doctors of the Catholic Church. Jesus gifted her with many visions, a supernatural wedding band, and the Stigmata; the latter two were visible only to her. She was a social activist, convincing Pope Gregory XI to move the papacy back to Rome, Italy from Avignon, France in 1377. Catherine would leave the world an impressive collection of her prayers, 400+ letters, and her famous work, *The Dialogue*, detailing her conversation with God during a time of spiritual ecstasy.

† "Feast Day in Rome" was inspired while praying at the Basilica di Santa Maria Sopra Minerva (Basilica of Our Lady over Minerva), where I visited on her feast day. The name (Our Lady above Minerva) speaks to the archeology of the church, as the building and accompanying convent were built over three ancient Roman temples: "the Minervium, of Domitian originally erected in honor of Minerva Chalkidiki, Iseum dedicated to Isis and Serapeum dedicated to Serapis."[23] Her

devotional chapel (accessed via the sacristy) was constructed from the room where Catherine died.[24] The crypt gate was open for all to enter and touch her sarcophagus. The Holy Spirit gifted me with the word contemplation.

Feast Day in Rome

cold stone tomb feels slick, soft
on my warm palm
pumping with blood

cupping the sculpted hand
she speaks to me:
touch me
feel me
read me
know me

contemplation increases
explanation as
tranquil ecstasy
w r i t h e s
i n
d i s c o u r s e,
apologetics
lettres, all inside
her ring of flesh

She Is

a flare of truth rising, shining
amongst ecclesial filth
administering Eucharist
whose eternities rest in Dantean
circles

she is
her interior cell,
moving mountains of papal
discord home to Rome,
the roots of her obedience
extending into the soil of social
reform

she is
uncommon to her genus,
holy anorexic, lavished in
stings from straps with hooks
bringing budding flowers
open wounds
on taut skin

she is
a Dominican she-wolf
protecting her harried
young from hounds'
infectious bites of luxury

Teresa of Avila

Feast Day, October 15

Also known as Saint Teresa of Jesus (1515-1582) this Spanish mystic and Doctor of the Church would remain physically ill yet spiritually strong most of her life. A Sister of the Carmelite Convent of the Incarnation at Avila, she would be graced with supernatural visions and other mystical experiences. Some of her most profound works include her *Autobiography* and *The Interior Castle*; each demonstrates an exquisite example of the personal life of a mystic intimately connected with God, one that knows mystical ecstasy well. Teresa would go on to found the Discalced Carmelites.

Notable is that Teresa is an incorruptible saint. Her post-mortem body was found incorruptible, her heart still displaying the transverberation marks.

† "Doctor and Physician" was inspired while praying at La Farmacia di Santa Maria della Scala (The Apothecary of Holy Mary of the Staircase), where I saw Saint Teresa's encased foot.

If you see Father Rudolf, tell him I said hello—this priest is one of the most intelligent, delightful, helpful men of God I met while in Rome! The Holy Spirit gifted me with the words iconic and healing.

Doctor and Physician

for Padre Rudolf

I keep your secrets,
your words
wholly breathing, wise
inside my
mind

my castle holds
your remedy of riches, your tunnel
deepens the rivers running through
my ventricles,
theological sutures
remain, move, speaking softly
under my skin

my fragile feet find
hard ground,
rock rises from the sinking sand
your holy corpus
incorrupts my body

my iconic prayer is exposed
everywhere:
I have no shame

in the kitchen,
at the dinner table,
during a meeting
in prayer

my painful ache
my ecstasy
will ignite Bernini's flame
healing hearts of
all who gaze upon
my white
marble flesh

In Her Words[25]

The greatest perfection attainable along the spiritual path lies in this conformity: Sisters, how important it was to win previous battles.

The silkworms come from seeds about the size of little grains of pepper.

Courage, my daughters! Weave this little cocoon by getting rid of our self-love and self-will, our attachment to earthly things.

It is necessary for the silkworm to die

If the locutions come from the imagination, neither certitude, nor peace, nor interior delight—as ours will not understand his grandeurs.

The natural heat fails, and the fire burns the soul. Courage is necessary. Are you able to drink the chalice?

Sound Bites

digression is good for a doctor
with favor,
as

decades of collected, heady
knowledge occurs
spontaneously

discombobulation threads
normality in honest
business and, *why does this matter, Lord?*
creation is just that: mystic, and
who will this help, really?

humility breeds the poetic heart,
its hedge of protection,
laughter,
its enemy,
an inflated mediating
ego out of balance

Thérèse of Lisieux

Feast Day, October 1

The youngest Doctor of the Church, Thérèse (1873-1897) entered religious life at age fifteen. For such a short life, she made an enormous impact, teaching that love is what truly matters above all else. Because of this attitude, she was known to surround herself with less lovable Sisters, serving them in love and peace. She practiced simplicity of faith, and wore well the appellation "Little Flower of Jesus." It is said that a rose bush bloomed as she was dying, and then a rain of roses fell following her passing. Still today, there have been accounts of miraculous appearances of roses or the fragrance of roses in association with her veneration. In addition to her other writings, Thérèse's autobiographical work *Story of a Soul* continues to be a global bestseller, translated into over 60 dialects and languages.[26]

† "Visiting Hours" was inspired while visiting the Bishops' Office for United States Visitors to the Vatican. It is here where I met the ever-joyful Fr. Leo; Sr. Mary Christa Nutt, RSM; and, Sr. Mary Juanita Gonsalves, RSM, all true servants of God. This poem is dedicated to Sr. Mary Juanita. The Holy Spirit gifted me with the word fresh.

Visiting Hours

For Sr. Mary Juanita
Sister of Mercy, Rome

an exuding light amongst
Rome's rubble, a feminine voice
amongst patriarchal stubble,
she lights the city
with memory,
decency, creativity,
maturity

a gift of glee,
on Christmas Eve
the scent of a rose
wafting during a fresh May breeze,

her prayer lifted up
1:11 timestamped
before her nap in her field
of flowers

Bike Riding with Maurice

summer
sun quickly
fades into the gloaming

days get shorter
fireflies signal sets
of seasons
listening to the Father
in loving discernment

a welcomed penance of
scraped knees and elbows,
tears bringing
tender love,

twinned, youthful
souls,
sibling love
remembers

to desire vinegar to
honey, to see
the good
in the bad and the ugly

III

FORERUNNERS

I understand three ways of contemplating motherhood in God. The first is the foundation of our nature's creation; the second is his taking of our nature, where the motherhood of grace begins; the third is the motherhood at work. And in that, by the same grace, everything is penetrated…and it is all one love.

~ Julian of Norwich, *Showings*

E lizabeth

Feast Day, November 5

Cousin of Mary (Mother of Jesus), Elizabeth carried in her womb the cousin of the Christ Child. During Mary's visit, the child growing inside Elizabeth's womb leapt at Mary's greeting to her cousin—most likely confirmation that the Holy Spirit filled John prior to his birth. At this leap in faith, Elizabeth proclaims to Mary, "Blessed are you who believed that what was spoken to you by the Lord would be fulfilled."[27]

Also substantial is the time of year of Elizabeth's pregnancy. John's Nativity is celebrated on June 24, the Summer Solstice. After this date, the days become shorter. Jesus's Nativity is celebrated on December 25th (for Orthodox Christians, around January 7), after which the days become longer. Here, we find one (John) must decrease in order for the other (Jesus) to increase.[28]

Another important factor is that the person of John straddles two worlds: Jewish and Christian. He assists in the entrance of Jesus, the Christ, into the world. And this comes about all because Elizabeth made the choice to be obedient to God, to carry her child late in her life.

† "Summer Solstice" was inspired while praying at the Basilica of San Silvestro in Capite (Basilica of Saint Sylvester the First), where I saw Saint John the Baptist's head. The Holy Spirit gifted me with the phrase, help me.

Summer Solstice

distracted constantly:
Mommy Brain hits early
so much to do:
waiting wash,
wild weeds, a n d
those *help me, Lord,* in-laws,

he's active in her watery womb
a sign, she thinks, of
a healthy baby with, um

personality

midwife's time
to move in

it's warming, but winter's
coming

M ary, Blessed Virgin

Feast Days, January 1 (Solemnity); March 25 (Annunciation); August 15 (Assumption); December 8 (Immaculate Conception)

The Blessed Virgin Mary is the mother of Jesus Christ. Mary carries many designations such as Theotokos, Blessed Mother, Queen of Heaven, and Madonna. Tradition presents three different birth sites for this young Jewish mother of God: Bethlehem, Sephoris, and (most likely) Jerusalem.[29] When the Virgin was approximately twelve or thirteen, the angel Gabriel came to her, telling her she would become pregnant via the power of the Holy Spirit. Joseph, her betrothed, doubted her story until he received an angelic visitation corroborating her account.

Mary's importance is paramount to Christ's ministry: she birthed Him; she helped to inaugurate His ministry at the wedding of Cana; and, she was present at His crucifixion. Her global popularity is immense; multitudes of Christians venerate her, praying for her intercession.

Two events during Mary's life should be well-noted: The Immaculate Conception and her Assumption. Mistakenly, many think the Immaculate Conception refers to when Mary conceived Jesus. The Immaculate Conception actually refers to the conception of Mary while living in her mother Anna's womb. Church dogma professes that Mary was exempt from Original Sin, a flawed condition all other humans possess (and can be cleansed from via the sacrament of baptism). This special exemption means sin never entered Mary's soul upon her animation as a person. Even though she is excused from Original Sin, she is not a deity. She was human, and therefore in need of Christ's salvific offer in order to serve as His mother. Also, because she was human, Mary would have known human experiences such as physical pain, emotional expression, and human death.[30]

Speaking of experiencing death, Mary's Assumption signifies her departure from Earth into Heaven. Although the exact year, location, and even Dormition experience cannot be precisely determined, East and West Church traditions agree that Mary's tomb was empty when opened. Tradition holds that it was none other than (doubting) Thomas who requested her tomb be opened (see St. John's *De Obit S. Dominae*). For the apostles, especially those present at her burial, her empty tomb evidenced the Mother of Christ's assumption into Heaven.

† "Motherhood" was inspired while praying at the Basilica di Santa Maria Maggiore (the Basilica of Saint Mary Major), where I saw slats from Jesus's trough (crib). The Holy Spirit gifted me with the word busy. A healthy number of Catholic churches in Rome are consecrated to Mary; St. Mary Major is the largest. Also notable is the plethora of grottos devoted to Mary around Rome; you can find them attached to buildings, city walls, inside churches, and even inside train stations!

Motherhood

for Fr. Pablo Migone

"Okay, Kiddo, let's go."
walking down the temple
steps into my busy day,
I stop,
turning to watch him
hop down the steps,
one-by-one,
behind me, just beyond the
reach of my hemline

I reach my hand for his.
he offers both,

raising him to
my hip, I select this moment
to remember his brown
eyes, sweet and wide,

his brown
skin, the color of wheat, kissably mine

too soon he will grow
into the burden of
his identity

Protoevangelium

I intentionally stepped on your head,
sinlessly strolling
on my way to Joe's
on my way to tell him the news

And, you know, I honestly thought you would

react differently,   at my strike
you didn't even curve, coil, or hiss

not like when
we knew each other before:
handsome to my eyes
longing to my heart
persuasive to my ears
tasty to my flesh

your essence, your squishiness between
my toes
feels refreshing…ly powerful

and emancipating

your blood and guts and scales warm
my flesh pressing against cool sandy mud
juxtaposed against the midday sun
kissing the top of my arch

my seed, my seed, my seed
expressing her full man
speaks into time prior
while
I walk on

Mary Magdalene

Feast Day, July 22

Known as The Apostle to the Apostles, Saint Mary Magdalene (or, Mary of Magdala) held several roles: the first witness to Jesus Christ's Resurrection, evangelist, and saint. Placing Mary's witness as a woman to the Resurrection in context is important. During that time, most women were less than second class citizens. Their opinions and testimonies, especially in formal settings like court, were utterly irrelevant. Therefore, for Jesus to choose Mary—a previously demonically tormented public outcast who was societally worthless due to her gender—as the first person to see Him alive after His death would have been wholly unthinkable.[31]

Her testimony served as an example of Christianity's very foreign approach to the value of women as compared to other religions and governmental principalities in the region. These pro-female teachings created an avenue for many women to follow Christ, and experience the love and respect they had been denied their entire lives.

After the Christian expulsion, Mary is known to have spent her last 30 years "in a cavern of a rock, La Sainte Baume, high up among the Maritime Alps, to be transported miraculously, just before she died, to the chapel of St. Maximim."[32] Another account suggests her body is buried near Mary's house (Mother of Jesus) in Ephesus.[33] Either way, Saint Mary Magdalene played and continues to play a crucial role in the narrative of Christianity.

† "Beauty" was inspired while praying at Basilica di S. Giovanni Battista dei Fiorentini (Basilica of Saint John the Baptist of Florence [in Rome]), where her foot/relic is located. The Holy Spirit gifted me with the word chilled.

Beauty

a fragile lily,
sometimes still chilled
by callous accusations from the
so-called pious folk in town,
I awake to the morning sun,
clothed in your love,

my body, your temple

I am the new genuine article:
liberated
recreated
impregnated
with new life
growing in my barren areas

my arms stretch into your light,
the ichthus tattooed on my wrist
reminds me of our passionate,
compassionate
commitment

stepping out into the light
my weathered soles kiss soft, worn
ground leading me back to the garden,

divinely fresh, offering olives of agony and
crimson fruit

Priscilla

Feast Day, July 8

Patron saint of good marriages, Priscilla (also called Prisca) is commonly identified with Priscilla in the New Testament. She and her husband Aquila are thought to have worked as tent-making merchants. She was a friend and mentee of the Apostle Paul, and has been viewed as an apostle, pastor, church planter, evangelist, missionary, and teacher of the Jewish-Christian evangelist, Apollos. In some theological circles, Priscilla is regarded as the author of the anonymous *Letter to the Hebrews*.[34] During their diaspora (Jews were forced to leave Rome by rule of the *Edict* of Claudius in the year 49CE), Priscilla and her husband lived in Corinth and Ephesus, evangelizing and converting people to the Way of Christ.

† "Rabbi" was inspired while praying at Santa Prisca (Saint Prisca), where the baptismal the apostle Peter used to baptize Prisca (Priscilla) is located. The Holy Spirit gifted me with the word baptism.

Rabbi

for X Winter

assessing the burdens of Diaspora
she sits, considering student
questions in context of the Christ,
pilgrimage, sacrifice, apostasy

three fingers massage
her smooth forehead, reflecting,
reasoning, ruminating late
into the night
baptized in prose,
carefully crafting words, composing
her answers, her letter
to her Abrahamic people
as witness
of her muse

IV

FOUNDRESSES

In the beginning there are a great many battles and a good deal of suffering for those who are advancing towards God…It is like those who wish to light a fire; at first they are choked by the smoke and cry, and by this means obtain what they seek (as it is said: 'Our God is a consuming fire' [Heb 12:24]): so we also must kindle the divine fire in ourselves through tears and hard work.

~ Amma Syncletica, Desert Mother[35]

B ridget of Sweden

Feast Day, July 23

Of noble birth to parents Birger Persson and Ingeborg Bengtsdotter and of noble marriage to Prince Ulf Gudmarsson, Saint Bridget or Brigitta (1303-1373) is the patron saint of Sweden and one of the Church's most beloved mystics. She was blessed with divine visions such as seeing Christ as the Man of Sorrows and receiving directive words to revivify the Church, the latter prompting her to found in 1344 what would become a global order now known as the Bridgettines. Although she never became a nun, she devoted her life to Christ; serving as His emissary, she received a plethora of visions, including those involving papal hierarchy.

† "Inked" was inspired while praying at Santa Brigida a Campo de' Fiori (Saint Bridget at the Field of Flowers). The Holy Spirit gifted me with the words cloistered and dialogue.

Inked

cloistered in my womb
of theology, birthed
to be your bride, your love,
your groove pens
my life,
scribe of your heart,
a writer's rhythm
breathing,
dialoguing

ordering

my words
in the stifling, sifting sand
sparkling in between my toes
twirling
to evening vespers

F austina

Feast Day, October 5

Polish born mystic, apostle, and prophet, Saint Faustina Kowalska (Faustyna Kowalski) of the Most Blessed Sacrament (1905-1938) is one of Christendom's most popular historical saints. A Sister of Our Lady of Mercy, Faustina helped young women experiencing great dysfunction in their lives. Several years after entering religious life, in the 1930s, she would receive a revelation from God instructing her to paint an image of Him, signing it "Jesus I trust in You."

Even though she secretly suffered from tuberculosis, she continued to show great mercy to others and experienced much spiritual delight, enjoying a mystical life of "apparitions, ecstasies, the gift of bilocation, hidden stigmata, reading into human souls, [and] the mystical betrothal and nuptials."[36] Her *Diary*, a globally significant text, has become a devotion to the Divine Mercy, and was termed by Saint John Paul II "a Gospel of Mercy written from a 20th century perspective."[37]

† "Intersession" was inspired while praying at Chiesa di Santo Spirito in Sassia (Church of the Holy Spirit in Saxony [the Saxon district]), where I experienced my own theophanic moment while gazing upon the miraculous painting of Jesus. This former hospital church that sits in Vatican City's shadow is one of the most lively we visited. Bustling with tourists, parishioners, and the Sisters of Mercy, activity is abound here— maybe this is why the church is dedicated to the Holy Spirit! There is a chapel devoted to Saint John Paul II that includes his relics. Wonderful is the ornamentation of rosaries and medals in the third chapel on the right dedicated to the Divine Mercy and Saint Faustina; these tributes are from families who, after having much trouble conceiving, prayed for intercession and became pregnant! A beautiful statue of Saint Faustina and her relics are also located in this chapel. A personal highlight was the 1992 Moskal rendition of the "Merciful Jesus," the famous image that Faustina envisioned. The Holy Spirit gifted me with the phrase, living god.

Intercession

Teenage girl walking
the pebbled trail.
At her side,
her trusted confidant weeps
with her in the steamy afternoon.

Rain approaches.

Heaving, heavy ominous
clouds accompany a calm,
silent womb
of thick air

broken, cracked words to
hang and swirl around the tiny
ridges inside her
elder's ear.

No word is good enough
today. The merciful
Sister remains silent,
sheds tears,
she's with her, that's all.

She intercedes to her living god,

listening on

as blades of fragile grass
sprouting in between
crumbling stone
wave in empathy.

She blinks back,
compassionate listener,
a private gesture well welcomed

F rances

Feast Day, March 9

Rome's patron saint and mystic, Frances or Francesca (1384-1440) lived a truly selfless life. Although she came from a noble family and married wealthy (her betrothal would include a partying, socialite mother-in-law!), she lived for Christ, giving away clothes, food, anything the poor needed. In fact, during a time of plague when people were starving, she gave away the family's food supply. But, to her displeased father-in-law and husband's surprise, the food and wine miraculously replenished itself! She even converted part of her house into a hospital during a time of plague.

Frances never complained, even though she faced a myriad of dismal challenges: extended illnesses, premature death of her sons and a daughter, an ill husband, ridicule from her community about her Christocentric lifestyle, war, and plague. She would found an order of oblate nuns, an order that helped the poor and needy. Frances experienced many miracles, prophesy (even her own death date!), and moments of mystical ecstasy in her life; she even saw her guardian angel.

† "Veneration" was inspired while praying at Santa Francesca Romana (Saint Frances of Rome, previously Santa Maria Nova), while I reflected upon her skeleton, adorned in her habit, and holding Holy Scripture in her hands. The breviary is open to Psalm 73. Tradition suggests due to tending to her husband one day, she was unable to complete her prayers. When she finally returned, this verse appeared in gold: "You have taken me by the right hand, and by your will you have led me, and with glory have received me." The Holy Spirit gifted me with the word bones.

Veneration

sing to me, Francesca
your bones bring
offerings:

pictures of children,
created from your intercession

signs of the cross,
aged hands, tic-tac
knuckles

knees on wood,
sore from the floor
tingling then numbing,
penance
engaging God

birds chirp outside while

you rest until the Parousia,
quietly waiting in your lighted glass box

H elena

Feast Day, August 18

Widely known as Saint Constantine's mother, this Empress (d. 330CE) started life as the daughter of an inn keeper. She married Constantius I Chlorus (a Roman general), only to be divorced later so that he could aspire to be Caesar by marrying Theodora, Emperor Maximian's stepdaughter.[38] But, before he could divorce her, she became pregnant with a boy (Constantine) who would become a famous emperor and liberator of the Christian people. During the 312 battle at the Milvian Bridge, Constantine saw the Chi Rho symbol—the first two letters of Christ's name—that would lead him to victory and to legalize Christianity just a year later through his 313 *Edict of Milan*.

Helena gave her life to help the poor. She established many churches and holy sites. In addition to her evangelization efforts, she made one of the first recorded archeological expeditions, one that would lead her to discover the True Cross; a piece of this cross instantaneously healed a deleteriously ill woman. In addition to the True Cross, Helena also brought back to Rome the nails used to affix Jesus to His Cross and the placard reading "King of the Jews." In honor of his mother, Emperor Constantine would mint currency in her name, Flavia Julia Helena.

† "Empress" was inspired while praying at Basilica di Santa Maria in Ara Coeli (Basilica of Saint Mary of the Alter of Heaven). Saint Helena's chapel is located to the left of the main altar, and is a rotunda; the dome is supported by pink marble columns. Tradition holds that Saint Frances of Rome levitated while praying in this chapel. Helena's relics are located in the urn. The Holy Spirit gifted me with the word exhaustive.

Empress

knees in the dirt,

this
inconvenient
wife

digs with furious care,
soil of Calvary smothers my lungs,
packs my nails,
encases my arms

then,
kneeling in the cool, earthen
cave, I encounter that rugged,
bloodied wood
resting in peace
under Juno's temple

aching ankles,
I stand, hands on thighs
wrist bone pockets popping

my inquiry, exhaustive,
an excavation of my heart

M onica

Feast Day, August 27

The patron saint of married women, mothers, alcoholics, and abused women, Monica (331-387CE) knew challenge well. Also known as Monica of Hippo (present day Algeria, Africa), she experienced a series of challenges: alcohol addiction during her youth; an un-believing, abusive husband; a belligerent mother-in-law; and, an extremely rebellious son. Through all of these stresses, Monica prayed and persevered. God would answer her prayers: her husband and mother-in-law eventually converted to Christianity; two of her children (Navigius and Perpetua) would enter religious life; and, with help from Ambrose, she would work to bring her recalcitrant son Augustine back to the faith. This restoration also helped to mend the relationship between mother and son. Monica would be praised and memorialized in Augustine's famed *Confessions*.

† "An African Angel" was inspired while praying at Basilica di Sant'Agostino (Basilica of Saint Augustine). An unassuming façade, anyone could walk by this basilica and not experience the treasures waiting inside. The Chapel of Saint Monica (left of the main alter) is a treasure trove filled with wonderful pieces: her original sarcophagus; her marble urn; another tomb just to

the left comprised with pieces from tombs of the past, including ones from the 15th and 16th centuries; frescoes depicting scenes from her life; paintings of her other children, Navigius and Perpetua; and, Vanitelli's restoration of *Our Lady of Consolation with Angels, St Augustine and St Monica*.[39] When we entered the church after the first morning Mass, incense still lingered in the air. Approaching her chapel, lively praises could be heard, as a small group of people were holding a special Mass in her chapel singing and praising the Lord—hands lifted high in the air. This church was thriving with the Holy Spirit, completely engulfed with Its presence. I could have stayed there all day. The Holy Spirit gifted me with the words alive and living.

An African Angel

confident in chaos
because
angst can't survive,
can't be alive
in a mother's prayers
against her son's
acid Manichean tongue
a machine of rhetoric,
philosophy
and *me*ology

birthed that child
his father's son,
kingdom come,
the Cain of the family
inheritance to carry
on, and yet
her living deity
would call him,
create in him
a friend

a mother's prayer
always takes care
her call, an agent
her greatness
communicates
elucidates
escalates
venerates

Him

Teresa of Calcutta

Feast Day, September 5

Born Agnes Gonxha Bojaxhiu in Skopje, Macedonia, Teresa of Calcutta (1910-1997) took her religious name after Thérèse of Lisieux. She entered the order of the Sisters of Loreto in Ireland at age eighteen. Then, stationed at St. Mary's School for Girls in Calcutta, India, she served as a teacher and, later, as principal.

In 1946, Mother Teresa received a call from God to serve the poor: "Jesus revealed His pain at the neglect of the poor, His sorrow at their ignorance of Him and His longing for their love"; in response, she was obedient to His call and founded the Missionaries of Charity in 1950, a community that would meet the needs "of the poorest of the poor."[40] Her obedience to this call would lead to an explosion of God's work. Teresa would be the recipient of many awards, including the 1962 Padmashri Award, the 1979 Nobel Peace Prize, and the 1985 United States' Presidential Medal of Freedom.

† "A Handful" was inspired while praying at Missionare della Carita (Missionaries of Charity), where Saint Teresa stayed while in Rome. At the Mission hangs a beautiful crucifix next

to the words "I Thirst"; from one angle, the crucifix covers the final "t," creating a poignant revelation. The Holy Spirit gifted me with the word handful. The second poem "Mother" is dedicated to Sister Victoria, a generous Sister serving at the Missionare della Carita in Rome.

A Handful

of love is all it takes
to quench the thirst of God
to evangelize his love,
her light,
she freely
gives to
souls who can only offer
bones showing
beneath thin layers of
skin

Mother

for Sr. Victoria, Missionary of Charity

she basks in the love
given from hundreds of little dirty
hands holding her worn blue hem,

she is
a Mary to call out to for a cup
of clean water in the night,

she is
a Joseph to cry out to for a shield
of safety in the midst of the frightening sound of flying
bullets

she is
a Thérèse to reach out to for a gentle
first hug, first trust of God, the Creator of nature

she is
a Jesus to pray to and talk with for the assurance
of an eternal life of love

About the Author

Circus Maximus. Rome, Italy. Photo by André Augusté.

Nicol Nixon Augusté, PhD, is a Professor of Liberal Arts. Her research interests include Women & Theology, Rhetoric & Composition, and Native American studies. Nicol is a SCAD American Academy in Rome Affiliated Fellowship recipient. Her work has appeared in journals such as *Sandhill Review* and *Catholic Medical Quarterly UK*, and *The Tau*. *Rome's Female Saints: A Poetic Pilgrimage to the Eternal City* stems from her passion for telling the stories of underrepresented women.

This book connects past, present, and future. Early followers of the Way, now known as Christians, have been and continue to be persecuted and martyred because of their faith in Jesus Christ. Please pray and stand in solidarity with me and with those who continue to be persecuted and martyred for their faith. And please pray their executioners will come to know God.

For more information and photos, visit me on Facebook at https://www.facebook.com/romesfemalesaints/ or email me at romesfemalesaints@gmail.com

Notes

1 Santamaria, Rev. Jerome. "The Fullness of the Law in Christ's Sermon on the Mount." Lecture. The Bishop's Office for U. S. Visitors to the Vatican. 19 April 2016.

2 Wuerl, Card. Donald, *The Martyrs: A Reflection on the Supreme Christian Witness* (Steubenville: Emannus Road, 2015) 5.

3 Saunders, Father William, "The Process of Becoming a Saint." (Arlington Catholic Herald. Catholic Education Resource Center).

4 Ibid.

5 Ibid.

6 Bowersock, G.W., *Martyrdom and Rome* (New York: Cambridge UP, 1995) 5.

7 Lemire, Paula Anne Sharkey, "The White Martyrdom of Kateri Tekakwitha (Catholic Online).

8 Aquilina, Mike. *The Witness of Early Christian Women: Mothers of the Church.* Huntington: Our Sunday Visitor, Inc., 2014. 44-45.

9 Ibid. 45-46.

10 Rev. Fr. Antonio Gallonio, *Tortures and Torments of the Christian Martyrs* (Los Angeles: Feral, 2004) 9, 174.

11 Saunders, Fr. William. "Church Teachings on Relics." *Arlington Catholic Herald.* Catholic Education Resource Center. 2003. Web. http://www.

catholiceduation.org/en/culture/catholic-contributions/the-process-of-becoming-a-saint.html

[12]   Roberts, Michael. *Poetry and the Cult of the Martyrs: The Liber Peristephanon of Prudentius* (Ann Arbor: U of Michigan P, 1993) 14, 16.

[13]   Saunders, "Church Teaching on Relics" (CERC)

[14]   Butler, Alban. *Butler's Lives of the Saints*. 2nd ed. 4 Vols. (Burns and Oats, 1956) 256.

[15]   *St. Agatha of the Goths*. Church pamphlet. English Edition. Rome, Italy: Sant'Agatha dei Goti, 2016.

[16]   Kirby, Fr. Jeffrey, S.T.L. *101 Surprising Facts about St. Peter's and the Vatican*. Charlotte: Saint Benedict, 2015.

[17]   Janos, Fr. S. Trans. "The Holy Women Martyrs Basilissa and Anastasia." Fr. S. Janos. 1996-2001. Web. 6 June 2016. http://www.holytrinityorthodox.com/calendar/los/April/15-02.htm

[18]   Koren, Antonio. "Sant 'Antonina of Nicea: Martyr." *Santi Beati e Testimoni*. 2001. Web. 26 August. 2016. http://www.santiebeati.it/dettaglio/51800

[19]   "Saint Antonina of Nicaea." *CatholicSaints.Info*. 7 June 2016. Web. 26 August 2016. http://catholicsaints.info/saint-antonina-of-nicaea/

[20]   Ibid.

[21]   Tucker, Mildred Anna Rosalie and Hope Malleson, *Handbook to Christian and Ecclesiastical Rome*. London: Adam and Charles Black, 1900. 277.

[22]   "'Sistine Chapel of the Middle Ages' Reopens to Public in Rome. Web. 23 March, 2016. Reuters http://mobile.reuters.com/article/lifestyleMolt/idUSKCN0WP1A2

23   "History of the Basilica of Santa Maria sopra Minerva." *Santa Maria sopra Minerva*. Web. http://www.santamariasopraminerva.it/storia.html

24   Thelen, Daniel, *Saints in Rome and Beyond!* Web. 5 April. 2016. www.saintsinrome.com

25   St. Teresa of Avila. Trans. Kieran Kavanaugh and Otilio Rodreguez. *The Interior Castle*. Study Edition Washington: Institute of Carmelite Studies, 2010.

26   "Saint Therese, 'The Little Flower." Society of the Little Flower: *Spreading Devotion to St. Thérèse of Lisieux*. 2016. Society of the Little Flower. Web 23 August 2016. http://www.littleflower.org/therese/

27   Luke 1:45. *The Catholic Study Bible*. Second Ed. NAB. Oxford UP, 2001.

28   John 3:30

29   Maas, Anthony. "The Blessed Virgin Mary." *The Catholic Encyclopedia*. Vol. 15. New York: Robert Appleton Company, 1912. 18 Aug. 2016. http://www.newadvent.org/cathen/15464b.htm.

30   Aquilina, Mike. *The Witness of Early Christian Women: Mothers of the Church*. Huntington: Our Sunday Visitor, Inc., 2014. 37.

31   Butler, v3, 162.

32   "Immaculate Conception." *New Advent*. 11 November 2017. www.newadvent.org/cathen/07674d.htm

33   Thelen, Daniel.

34   Hoppin, Ruth. *Priscilla's Letter: Fining the Author of the Epistle to the Hebrews* (Fort Bragg, CA: Lost Coast, 2009)

35   Swan, Laura. *The Forgotten Desert Mothers: Sayings, Lives, and Stories of Early Christian Women.* New York: Paulist, 2001.

36   "Biography." *The Congregation of the Sisters of Our Lady of Mercy.* Web. 17 July 2016. https://www.faustyna.pl/zmbm/en/biography/

37   Ibid.

38   Butler, v3, 346.

39   *The Basilica of Saint Augustine in Campus Martius and the Former Friary Complex.* Trans. Fr. Martin Nolan. (Rome: Trimsdale, 1992) 29, 30, 31.

40   "Bl. Teresa of Calcutta." *Catholic Online.* http://www.catholic.org/saints/saint.php?saint_id=5611

Appendix

Sites of Interest

VISITING ROME

Bishops' Office for United States Visitors to the Vatican

Address: Casa Santa Maria, Pontifical North American College

30 Via dell'Umilita

Phone: 011 39 06 690-011

Website: https://www.pnac.org/visitorsoffice/about-the-visitors-office/

NOTE: If you are planning to attend Papal Audiences or Masses (or if you are a newlywed couple desiring to have your marriage blessed), please contact your local diocese for tickets or the Office at visitorsoffice@pnac.org.

SEVEN PILGRIMAGE CHURCHES

Basilica of Saint Mary Major (Basilica di Santa Maria Maggiore)

Address: 42 Piazza di S. Maria Maggiore, 00100

Phone: 06 698 86800

Website: http://www.vatican.va/various/basiliche/sm_maggiore/index_en.html

Papal Basilica of St. Peter in the Vatican (Basilica Papale di San Pietro in Vaticano)

Address: Piazza San Pietro, 00120. Vatican City

Phone 06 6982

Website: http://www.vatican.va/various/basiliche/san_pietro/index_it.htm

Papal Basilica of Saint Paul outside the Walls (Basilica Papale San Paolo Fuori Le Mura)

Address: 1 Piazzale San Paolo, 00146

Phone: 06 6988 0800

Website: http://www.basilicasanpaolo.org/

Basilica of the Holy Cross in Jerusalem (Basilica di S. Croce in Gerusalemme)

Address: Piazza di Santa Croce in Gerusalemme, 00185

Phone: 06 7061 3053

Website: http://www.santacroceroma.it/en/

Basilica of Saint Sebastian outside the Walls (San Sebastiano fuori le Mura)

Address: 136 Via Appia Antica

Phone: 06 7887035

Basilica of Saint Lawrence outside the Walls (Basilica di San Lorenzo fuori le Mura)

Address: 3 Piazzale del Verano, 00185

Phone: 06 491511

Website: https://www.basilicadisanlorenzo.com/

Archbasilica of Saint John Lateran (Arcibasilica Papale di San Giovanni in Laterno)

Address: 4 Piazza di S. Giovanni in Laterno, 00184

Phone: 06 6988 6433

Website: http://www.vatican.va/various/basiliche/san_giovanni/index_it.htm

Sites Associated with Female Saints

Agatha

St. Agatha of the Goths (Sant'Agata dei Goti)

16 Via Mazzarino

Phone: 06 4893 0456

† Relic Site

Basilica of Saint Stephen in the Round (Basilica di Santo Stefano al Monte Celio)

7 Via Santo Stefano Rotondo

Phone: 06 4211 9130

Saint Agatha in Trastevere (Sant'Agata in Trastevere)

9 Largo San Giovanni de Matha

Phone: 06 580 3717

Agnes

St. Agnes at the Circus Agonalis (Sant'Agnese in Agone)

30 Via di Santa Maria dell'Anima/ Piazza Navona

Phone 06 6819 2134

† Relic Site

St. Agnes outside the Walls (Sant'Agnese fuori le Mura)

349 Via Nomentana, 00162

Phone: 06 8620 5456

Website: www.santagnese.org

✝ Relic Site

<small>ANASTASIA OF ROME AND BASILISSA OF ROME</small>
Our Lady of Peace (Santa Maria della Pace)
Address: 5 Vicolo del Arco della Pace, 00186
Phone 06 686 1156
✝ Relic Site

Papal Basilica of St. Peter in the Vatican (Basilica Papale di San Pietro in Vaticano)
Address: Piazza San Pietro, 00120. Vatican City
Phone 06 6982
Website: http://www.vatican.va/various/basiliche/san_pietro/index_it.htm

Gardens of Vatican City (Horti Civitatis Vaticanae)
Address: Vatican City
Phone: 06 6988 4676
Website: http://www.vaticanstate.va/content/vaticanstate/en/monumenti/giardini-vaticani.html

<small>ANASTASIA OF SIRMIUM</small>
Basilica of Saint Anastasia (Basilica di Sant'Anastasia al Palatino)
Address: 1 Piazza di S. Anastasia, 00186
Phone: 06 678 2980

<small>ANTONINA OF NICAEA</small>
Church of Saint Blaise of Armenia (Chiesa di San Biagio degli Armeni/ Chiesa di San Biaglio della Pagnotta)

Address: 63 Via Giulia
Phone: 06 6880 4891
† Relic Site

Saint Barbara of the Booksellers (Santa Barbara dei Librari)
Address: 186 Largo dei Librai, 00186
Phone: 06 718 8626

Parish of Saint Barbara at Capannelle (Parrocchia Santa Barbara alle Capannelle)
Address: 5 Via Settingiano 00178
Phone: 06 718 8626
Website: http://www.santabarbaracapannelle.it/contatti-e-orari/

Saint Bridget at the Field of Flowers (Santa Brigida a Campo de' Fiori)
Address: 96 Piazza Farnese
Phone: 06 6889 2596
Website: http://www.brigidine.org/

Basilica of Saint Paul outside the Walls (Basilica Papale San Paolo Fuori Le Mura)
Address: 1 Piazzale San Paolo, 00146
Phone: 06 6988 0800
Website: http://www.basilicasanpaolo.org/

Saint Lawrence in Panisperna (San Lorenzo in Panisperna)
Address: 90 Via Panisperna, 00184

Phone: 06 48 3667

CATHERINE OF SIENA
Basilica di Our Lady above Minerva (Basilica of Santa Maria sopra Minerva)
Address: 42 Piazza della Minerva 42 / 35 Via del Beato Angelico 35, 00186
Phone: 06 6992 0384
Website: http://www.santamariasopraminerva.it/
† Relic Site

CECILIA
Saint Cecilia in Trastevere (Santa Cecilia in Trastevere)
Address: 22 Piazza di Santa Cecilia, 00153
Phone: 06 4549 2739
† Relic Site

The Catacombs of Saint Callixtus (Callisto)
Address: 110/126 Via Appia Antica, 00179
Phone: 06 513 0151
Website: http://www.catacombe.roma.it/en/catacombe.php

CIRILLA/CYRILLA
Basilica of Saint Mary in Cosmedim (Basilica of Santa Maria in Cosmedin)
Address: 18 Piazza della Bocca della Verità, 00186
Phone: 06 678 7759
† Relic Site

ELIZABETH

Basilica of Saint Sylvester the First (Basilica di San Silvestro in Capite)

Address: 17A Piazza di S. Silvestro, 00187

Phone: 06 697 7121

† Relic Site

Ancient Saint Mary's (Santa Maria Antiqua)

Address: 1 Largo Romolo e Remo (Roman Forum), 00186

Phone: 06 3996 7700

FAUSTINA

Church of the Holy Spirit in the Saxon District (Chiesa di Santo Spirito in Sassia)

Address: 12 Via dei Penitenzieri

Phone: 06 687 9310

Website: http://www.divinamisericordia.it/

† Relic Site

FELICITY

Saint Susanna (Santa Susanna)

Address: 14 Via Venti Settembre, 00187

Phone: 06 4201 3734

Website: http://www.santasusanna.it/Objects/Home1.asp

† Relic Site

FRANCES/FRANCESCA (PATRON SAINT OF ROME)

Saint Frances of Rome (Santa Francesca Romana, previously Santa Maria Nova)

Address: 4 Piazza di Santa Francesca, 00186

Phone: 06 679 5528
† Relic Site

Helena
Basilica of Saint Mary of the Altar of Heaven (Basilica of Santa Maria in Ara Coeli)
Address: 12 Scala dell'Arc Capitolina, 00186
Phone: 06 6976 3839
† Relic Site

Basilica of the Holy Cross in Jerusalem (Basilica di S. Croce in Gerusalemme)
Address: Piazza di Santa Croce in Gerusalemme, 00185
Phone: 06 7061 3053
Website: http://www.santacroceroma.it/en/
† Relic Site

Julitta
Ancient Saint Mary's (Santa Maria Antiqua)
Address: 1 Largo Romolo e Remo (Roman Forum), 00186
Phone: 06 3996 7700

Mary Magdalene
Saint John the Baptist of the Florentines (San Giovanni Battista dei Fiorentini)
Address: 2 Via Acciaioli, 00186
Phone: 06 6889 2059
Website: http://www.sangiovannideifiorentini.net/
† Relic Site

Saint Mary Magdalene in Marzio Feild (Santa Maria Maddalena in Camp Marzio)
Address: 53 Piazza della Maddalena
Phone: 06 89 9281
Website: http://www.vicariatusurbis.org/?page_id=188&ID=896

Mary, Mother of God
Basilica of Saint Mary Major (Basilica di Santa Maria Maggiore)
Address: 42 Piazza di S. Maria Maggiore, 00100
Phone: 06 698 86800
Website: http://www.vatican.va/various/basiliche/sm_maggiore/index_en.html
† Relic Site

Monica
Basilica of Saint Augustine (Basilica di Sant'Agostino)
Address: 19 Via di Sant'Eustachio, 00186
Phone: 06 686 5334
† Relic Site

Prisca / Priscilla
Saint Prisca (Santa Prisca)
Address: 11 Via di Santa Prisca, 00153
Phone: 06 574 3798
Website: https://www.santaprisca.it/index.php?lang=en
† Relic Site

Catacomb of Priscilla
430 Via Salaria 00199
Phone: 06 8620 6272

Site: http://www.catacombepriscilla.com

SERAPHIA AND SABINA
Basilica of Saint Sabina at the Aventine (Basilica di Santa Sabina all'Aventino)
Address: 1 Piazza Pietro D'Illiria, 00153
Phone: 06 57 9401
✝ Relic Site

SUSANNA
Saint Susanna (Santa Susanna)
Address: 14 Via Venti Settembre, 00187
Phone: 06 4201 3734
Website: http://www.santasusanna.it/Objects/Home1.asp
✝ Relic Site

TERESA OF AVILA
Our Lady of the Staircase (Santa Maria della Scala)
Address: 22 Piazza della Scala, 00153
Phone: 06 580 6233
✝ Relic Site

Our Lady of Victory (Santa Maria della Vittoria)
Address: 17 Via Venti Settembre, 00187
Phone: 06 4274 0571
Website: http://www.chiesasantamariavittoriaroma.it/
✝ Relic Site

Saint Teresa of Avila (Santa Teresa d' Avila)
Address: 37 Corso d'Italia, 00198

Phone: 8742 0568

Website: http://parrocchiasantateresadavila.it/la-basilica.html

Teresa of Calcutta

Missionary Sisters of Charity (Suore Missionare della Carità)

Address: Salita di S. Gregorio, 00184

Phone: 06 700 8435

Website: http://www.motherteresa.org/layout.html

† Relic Site

Vittoria

Our Lady of Victory (Santa Maria della Vittoria)

Address: 17 Via Venti Settembre, 00187

Phone: 06 4274 0571

Website: http://www.chiesasantamariavittoriaroma.it/

† Relic Site

Consulted Works

Affanni, Anna Maria and Marina Cogotti Rossella Vodret. "Santa Susanna and San Bernardo All Terme." *Art and Culture Programme—Churches*. (Rome, Italy. Fratelli Palombi, 1993.) 35-42.

"Agnes Virgin and Martyr-St. Ambrose." *Crossroads Initiative*. 19 January 2016. Web. 13 July 2016. https://www.crossroadsinitiative.com/media/articles/agnesvirginandmartyr/

Aquilina, Mike. *The Witness of Early Christian Women: Mothers of the Church*. Huntington: Our Sunday Visitor, Inc., 2014.

As Romans Do: The Church of Santa Susanna in Rome: A Complimentary Guide to Rome. Community of Santa Susanna. 2010-2012.

Augustine. *Confessions*. Trans Albert Outler. (New York: Barns and Noble, 2007). 9.9.22.

"Baring-Gould's Lives of the Saints—Saint Tryphonia, Widow, Martyr, 3rd Century." *Lives of the Saints*, 1872. CatholicSaints. info. 18 October 2013. Web. 16 August 2016. http://catholicsaints.info/baring-goulds-lives-of-the-saints/

"Basilica/Church of Santa Anastasia al Palatino (Palatine Hill)." RomeTour.org 1 July 2011. Web. http://rometour.org/basilica-church-santa-anastasia-al-palatino-palatine-hill.html

The Basilica of Saint Augustine in Campus Martius and the Former Friary Complex. Trans. Fr. Martin Nolan. (Rome, Italy: Trimsdale, 1992). 29, 30, 31.

"Biography." *The Congregation of the Sisters of Our Lady of Mercy.* Web. 17 July 2016. https://www.faustyna.pl/zmbm/en/biography/

Bisconti, Fabrizio. "Human Torches Light the Night." Catholic Culture.org. 2016. *Trinity Communications.* Web. 28 August 2016.

"Bl. Teresa of Calcutta." *Catholic Online.* http://www.catholic.org/saints/saint.php?saint_id=5611

"The Blessed Virgin Mary." *Advent.* 2012 Kevin Knight. Web. 18 August 2016. http://www.newadvent.org/cathen/15464b.htm.

Bowersock, G.W. *Martyrdom and Rome.* New York: Cambridge UP, 1995.

Butler, Alban. *Butler's Lives of the Saints.* 2nd ed. 4 Vols. (Burns and Oats, 1956).

"Christmas Eve in Rome: Midnight Mass at Santa Maria in Ara Coeli (Free Italy Travel Advice)." *Dream of Italy.* 2002-2016. Web. https://dreamofitaly.com/2009/11/24/

new-christmas-eve-in-rome-midnight-mass-at-santa-maria-in-ara-coeli-free-italy-travel-advice/

Gallonio, Rev. Father Antonio. *Tortures and the Torments of the Christian Martyrs*. Los Angeles: Feral House, 2004.

Gihr, Rev. Nicholas. "The Saints of the Canon of the Mass." The Holy Sacrifice of the Mass. *The Catholic Voice*, 1918. Web http://www.sanctamissa.org/en/spirituality/saints-in-the-roman-canon.pdf

Hart, Vaughan and Peter Hicks, Trans. *Palladio's Rome: A Translation of Andrea Palladio's Two Guidebooks to Rome*. New Haven: Yale UP, 2006.

Hillesum, Etty. *An Interrupted Life and Letters from Westerbork*. New York: Holt, 1996.

"History of the Basilica of Santa Maria sopra Minerva." *Santa Maria sopra Minerva*. Web. http://www.santamariasopraminerva.it/storia.html

Hoppin, Ruth. *Priscilla's Letter: Finding the Author of the Epistle to the Hebrews*. Fort Bragg, CA: Lost Coast, 2009.

"Immaculate Conception." *New Advent*. 11 November 2017. www.newadvent.org/cathen/07674d.htm

"Interactive Floorplan." St. Peter's Basilica.info. Web. http://stpetersbasilica.info/floorplan.htm

Jacobs de Voragine. *The Golden Legend*. New York: Longmans, Green, and Co., 1941.

Janos, Fr. S. Trans. "The Holy Women Martyrs Basilissa and Anastasia." Fr. S. Janos. 1996-2001. Web. 6 June 2016. http://www.holytrinityorthodox.com/calendar/los/April/15-02.htm

Julian of Norwich. *Showings*. Trans. Edmund Colledge, O.S.A. and James Walsh, S.J.Mahwah, NJ: Paulist, 1978.

Kirby, Fr. Jeffrey, S.T.L. *101 Surprising Facts about St. Peter's and the Vatican*. Charlotte: Saint Benedict, 2015.

Kirsch, Johann Peter. "St. Felicitas." *The Catholic Encyclopedia*. Vol. 6. New York: Robert Appleton Company, 1909. 24 Aug. 2016 <http://www.newadvent.org/cathen/06028a.htm>.

Klemens, Loffer. "Saint Sabina." *Catholic Encyclopedia*. CatholicSaints.Info. 23 August 2014. Web 20 August 2016. <http://catholicsaitns.info/catholic-encyclopedia-saint-sabina/>

Koren, Antonio. "Sant 'Antonina of Nicea: Martyr." *Santi Beati e Testimoni*. 2001. Web. 26 August 2016. http://www.santiebeati.it/dettaglio/51800

Lemire, Paula Anne Sharkey. *The White Martyrdom of Kateri Tekakwitha*. Catholic Online. Web. http://www.catholic.org/featured/headline.php?ID=980

Maas, Anthony. "The Blessed Virgin Mary." *The Catholic Encyclopedia*. Vol. 15. New York: Robert Appleton Company, 1912. 18 August 2016. http://www.newadvent.org/cathen/15464b.htm.

MacArthur, John. *Twelve Extraordinary Women: How God Shaped Women of the Bible and What He Wants to Do with You.* (Nashville: Nelson, 2005). 174

McCulloch, Diarmaid. *Christianity: The First Three Thousand Years*. New York: Penguin, 2009.

"Notes about Your Extended Family in Heaven." *Catholicsaints. Info*. Web. http://catholicsaints.info/saint-anastasia-of-rome/

O'Carragain, Eamonn and Carol Neuman De Vegvar, Eds. *Roma Felix: Formation and Reflections of Medieval Rome*. Burlington, VT: Ashgate, 2007.

"Pictorial Lives of the Saints—Saint Seraphia, Virgin and Martyr." *CatholicSaints.Info* 20 August 2016. http://catholicsaints.info/pictorial-lives-of-the-saints-saint-seraphia-virgin-and-martyr/

"The Queen of the Catacombs." *Catacombs of Priscilla*. Web. 22 June, 2016. http://www.catacombepriscilla.com/index_en.html

"Readings for the Feast of S. Frances of Rome." *ICEL*. 2010 Web. August 18, 2016 http://www.liturgies.net/saints/francesofrome/readings.htm

Ricciotti, Giuseppe. *The Age of Martyrs: Christianity from Diocletian to Constantine*. Trans. Rev. Anthony Bull. Milwalkee: Bruce Publishing, 1959.

Roberts, Michael. *Poetry and the Cult of the Martyrs: The Liber Peristephanon of Prudentius*. Ann Arbor: U of Michigan P, 1993.

Romae, Mirabilia Urbis. *The Marvels of Rome*. New York: Italica, 1986.

"Saint Antonina of Nicaea." *CatholicSaints.Info*. 7 June 2016. Web. 26 August 2016. http://catholicsaints.info/ saint-antonina-of-nicaea/

"Santa Cirilla of Rome: Virgin and Martyr." *Santi Beati e Testimoni*. 22 October 2001. Web http://www.santiebeati.it/ dettaglio/90410

"Saint Cyrilla of Rome." *CatholicSaints.info*. 15 July 2012. Web. 16 August 2016. http://catholicsaints.info/saint-cyrilla-of-rome/

"Saint Therese, 'The Little Flower." *Society of the Little Flower: Spreading Devotion to St. Thérèse of Lisieux*. 2016. Society of the Little Flower. Web. 23 August 2016. http://www.littleflower. org/therese/

"Saint Victoria." *CatholicSaints.Info*. 10 July 20116. Web. 24 August 2016. http://catholicsaints.info/saint-victoria/

"'Sistine Chapel of the Middle Ages' Reopens to Public in Rome." Web. 23 March, 2016. Reuters. http://mobile.reuters. com/article/lifestyleMolt/idUSKCN0WP1A2

Santamaria, Rev. Jerome. "Reverse-Engineering Perfection: The Fullness of the Law in Christ's Sermon on the Mount." Lecture. Bishop's Office for United States Visitors. Rome, Italy. 19 April 2016.

Saunders, Fr. William. "Church Teaching on Relics." *Arlington Catholic Herald*. Catholic Education Resource Center. 2003. Web. http://www.catholiceducation.org/en/culture/catholic-contributions/the-process-of-becoming-a-saint.html

---. "The Process of Becoming a Saint." *Arlington Catholic Herald*. Catholic Education Resource Center. 2003. Web. http://www. catholiceducation.org/en/culture/catholic-contributions/the-process-of-becoming-a-saint.html

Scalzi, Padri Carmelitani. *Chiesa di Santa Maria della Vittoria*, Roma. Web. 25 August 2016. http://www. chiesasantamariavittoriaroma.it/

Sri, Edward P. "I Thirst": Mother Teresa's Devotion to the Thirst of Jesus. *Catholics United for the Faith*. November 2013. Web. 24 August 2016. Cited in Mother Teresa, *Where There is Love, There is God*, edited by Brian Kolodiejchuk, M.C., (New York: Image, 2010), 51. http://www.cuf.org/2014/01/ thirst-mother-teresas-devotion-thirst-jesus/

St. Agatha of the Goths. Church pamphlet. English Edition. Rome, Italy: Sant'Agatha dei Goti, 2016.

"St. Anastasia." *Catholic Online.* http://www.catholic.org/saints/ saint.php?saint_id=17 for the entire narrative

"St. Frances of Rome." *New Advent.* 2012. Kevin Knight. Web. 18 August 2016. http://www.newadvent.org/cathen/06205c.htm

"St. Monica." *Catholic Online.* 2016. Web. http://www.catholic. org/saints/saint.php?saint_id=1

"St. Prisca of Rome." *The Self-Ruled Antiochian Orthodox Christian Archdiocese of North America.* Web. 22 June 2016. www. antiochian.org/node/17335

"St. Priscilla, with Her Husband, Aquila, at Ephesus." *The Self-Ruled Antiochian Orthodox Christian Archdiocese of North America.* Web. 22 June 2016. www.antiochian.org/node/17511

Swan, Laura. *The Forgotten Desert Mothers; Saying, Lives, and Stories of Early Christian Women.* New York: Paulist, 2001.

Talbot, John Michael with Steve Rabey. *The Way of the Mystics: Ancient Wisdom for Experiencing God Today.* San Francisco: Jossey-Bass, 2005.

Thurston, Herbert. "Relics." *The Catholic Encyclopedia.* Vol. 12. New York: Robert Appleton Company, 1911. 6 July. 2016. http://www.newadvent.org/cathen/12734a.htm.

"Tuesday: Santa Prisca." *The Pontifical North American College.* Web. 22 June 2016. https://www.pnac.org/station-churches/ holy-week/tuesday-in-holy-week-santa-prisca/

Thelen, Daniel. *Saints in Rome and Beyond!* Web. 5 April. 2016. www.saintsinrome.com

Thurston, Herbert and Donald Attwater. *Butler's Lives of the Saints*. 4 vols. Allen, TX: Christian Classics, 1996.

Turker, Mildred Anna Rosalie and Hope Malleson. *Handbook to Christian and Ecclesiastical Rome*. (London: Adam and Charles Black, 1900). 277.

"Welcome." *Mother Teresa of Calcutta Center: Official Site*. Web. 23 August 2016. http://www.motherteresa.org/layout.html

Wuerl, Cardinal Donald. *To The Martyrs: A Reflection on the Supreme Christian Witness*. Steubenville: Emmaus, 2015.

Zimmerman, Benedict. "St. Teresa of Avila." *The Catholic Encyclopedia.*_Vol. 14. New York: Robert Appleton Company, 1912. 23 August. 2016. http://www.newadvent.org/cathen/14515b.htm.

CPSIA information can be obtained
at www.ICGtesting.com
Printed in the USA
LVHW020527290721
693949LV00008B/971

9 781512 781779